SHORT
PRAYERS
OF STRENGTH
FOR
Women

HARVEST HOUSE PUBLISHERS
EUGENE, OREGON

Short Prayers of Strength for Women
Copyright © 2021 by PLJ Communications
Published by Harvest House Publishers
Eugene, Oregon 97408
www.harvesthousepublishers.com

ISBN 978-0-7369-8204-7 (pbk.)
ISBN 978-0-7369-8205-4 (eBook)

Design by Peter Gloege | LOOK Design Studio

M is a federally registered trademark of the Hawkins Children's LLC.
Harvest House Publishers, Inc., is the exclusive licensee of the trademark.

Printed in the United States of America
21 22 23 24 25 26 27 28 29 / VP / 10 9 8 7 6 5 4 3 2 1

CONTENTS

FOR ME, PRAYER IS AN
ASPIRATION OF THE HEART,

IT IS A SIMPLE GLANCE
DIRECTED TO HEAVEN,

IT IS A CRY OF GRATITUDE
AND OF LOVE

IN THE MIDST OF TRIALS
AS WELL AS JOY;

FINALLY, IT IS SOMETHING GREAT,
SUPERNATURAL,

WHICH EXPANDS MY SOUL
AND UNITES ME TO JESUS.

—SAINT THERESE OF LISIEUX

ILLUMINATE MY MIND

AS I PONDER AND
PRAY IN THE
STILLNESS,
I DREAM AS A
DREAMER
OF DREAMS.

—AIMEE SEMPLE McPHERSON

I DO NOT KNOW, O GOD,

WHAT WILL **HAPPEN** TO ME TODAY.

I KNOW ONLY THAT

NOTHING WILL **HAPPEN** TO ME

BUT WHAT HAS BEEN FORESEEN

BY YOU FROM ALL **ETERNITY,**

AND THAT IS SUFFICIENT,

O MY GOD, TO KEEP ME IN **PEACE.**

I ADORE YOUR ETERNAL DESIGNS.

I SUBMIT TO THEM WITH

ALL MY HEART.

—ELISABETH OF FRANCE

POINT THE
DIRECTION, LORD.
YOUR SERVANT
IS READY
TO MOVE FORWARD.
AMEN.

· · · · · · · · · · ❧ · · · · · · · · · ·

HELP US TO BE **MINDFUL**
THAT WE ARE NOT ALONE.
WHEN WE NEED **WISDOM,**
WE NEED ONLY TO ASK FOR IT.
YOU HAVE **PROMISED**
TO BESTOW IT LIBERALLY....
TEACH US TO KNOW THAT
IF WE ARE TO BE SUCCESSFUL STEWARDS,
WE MUST BE YOUR **SERVANTS.**

—BARBARA JORDAN

DEAR GOD,
I HAVE SO MANY
WORRIES TODAY.
MAY I LEAVE THEM
WITH YOU?

———

I HAVE BEEN POURING OUT
MY SOUL BEFORE THE LORD.

—1 SAMUEL 1:15 ESV

OH, HELP ME, GOD!
FOR THOU ALONE
CANST MY DISTRACTED
SOUL RELIEVE;
FORSAKE IT NOT:
IT IS THINE OWN,
THOUGH WEAK,
YET LONGING TO BELIEVE.
OH, DRIVE THESE
CRUEL DOUBTS AWAY;
AND MAKE ME KNOW
THAT THOU ART GOD!
A FAITH, THAT SHINES
BY NIGHT AND DAY,
WILL LIGHTEN EVERY
EARTHLY LOAD.

—ANNE BRONTE
FROM "THE DOUBTER'S PRAYER"

O GOD,
PLEASE SHOWER YOUR WISDOM
ON THOSE LIVING IN CONFUSION
AND DARKNESS,
AND YOUR PEACE OF MIND
ON ALL WHO ARE TROUBLED.
AMEN.

PRAYER IS NOT MONOLOGUE,
BUT DIALOGUE;
GOD'S VOICE IS ITS
MOST ESSENTIAL PART.
LISTENING TO GOD'S VOICE
IS THE SECRET OF THE ASSURANCE
THAT HE WILL LISTEN TO MINE.

—ANDREW MURRAY

MAY I SEE
DIFFICULTY AS A
CHALLENGE,
A HOLY ERRAND.
A SIGN OF YOUR
CONFIDENCE IN ME,
IN *US*.
IN WHAT I CAN
OVERCOME
THROUGH YOUR
POWER AND
WISDOM.

AMEN.

BEHOLD, LORD...

MY WORLD IS FILLING

WITH DARKNESS,

WITH IGNORANCE.

TODAY MAY I OFFER

ALL OF THE

LIGHT AND TRUTH

THAT I CAN.

AMEN.

DEAR GOD,

WHEN I THINK IT'S **OVER**,
REMIND ME THAT IT'S **NOT OVER**.
AMEN.

❧

LET NOTHING FRIGHTEN YOU.
ALL THINGS PASS AWAY:
GOD NEVER CHANGES.
PATIENCE OBTAINS ALL THINGS.
THOSE WHO HAVE GOD
FIND THEY LACK NOTHING;
GOD ALONE SUFFICES.

—SAINT TERESA OF AVILA

DEAR GOD,
MAY I TREAT MY BODY,
MIND, AND SOUL
LIKE THEY BELONG
TO SOMEONE WHO
LOVES ME.
AMEN.

———

I TRY TO INCREASE THE POWER GOD HAS GIVEN ME

TO SEE THE BEST IN EVERYTHING AND EVERYONE,

AND MAKE THAT BEST A PART OF MY LIFE.

—HELEN KELLER

O GOD,

HELP ME TO

BELIEVE

THE TRUTH ABOUT

MYSELF,

NO MATTER HOW

BEAUTIFUL

IT IS!

—MACRINA WIEDERKEHR

LEAD ME

FROM THE UNREAL TO THE REAL,
LEAD ME FROM DARKNESS TO LIGHT,
LEAD ME FROM DEATH TO LIFE,
FROM FALSEHOOD TO TRUTH.
LEAD ME FROM DESPAIR TO HOPE,
FROM FEAR TO TRUST.
LEAD ME FROM HATE TO LOVE,
FROM WAR TO PEACE.
LET PEACE FILL OUR HEARTS,
OUR WORLD, OUR UNIVERSE.
PEACE. PEACE. PEACE.

—MOTHER TERESA

LORD OF ALL,
THANK YOU FOR THE
SACRED PRIVILEGE OF
BEING ALIVE.
ALIVE TO LOVE, TO SERVE,
TO SHARE, TO REJOICE.
AMEN.

———

ACT AND GOD WILL ACT,
WORK AND HE WILL WORK.

—SAINT JOAN OF ARC

MY ALL-KNOWING

CREATOR,

TODAY MAY I CHOOSE

MY WORDS WITH LOVE AND CARE,

TODAY MAY I LIFT THE SPIRITS

OF ANY WHO GRIEVE,

TODAY MAY I

BE WILLING TO FORGIVE

⫸⟶ AND ⟵⫷

TO ASK FORGIVENESS,

TODAY MAY I LEAD OTHERS

AS YOU HAVE LED ME.

AMEN.

—PAT LAWRENCE

LORD JESUS CHRIST,

I TURN MY THOUGHTS TO YOU.

I SET ASIDE ALL DISTRACTIONS

AND PREOCCUPATIONS.

I WILL FIND REST AND

PEACE AND DIRECTION

IN YOUR PRESENCE.

I CHERISH THIS CHANCE TO PRAY.

AMEN.

IF I CAN DO NOTHING ELSE,
I WILL PRAY.

—MARIANNE ADLARD

ALMIGHTY GOD,

WHO KNOWEST OUR NECESSITIES

BEFORE WE ASK,

AND OUR IGNORANCE IN ASKING:

SET FREE THY SERVANTS

FROM ALL ANXIOUS THOUGHTS

FOR THE MORROW;

GIVE US CONTENTMENT WITH

THY GOOD GIFTS.

—SAINT AUGUSTINE

THE END OF
A MATTER IS BETTER THAN
ITS BEGINNING, AND PATIENCE
IS BETTER THAN PRIDE.

—ECCLESIASTES 7:8

HEAVENLY FATHER,

HELP YOUR CHILDREN TO . . .

ENCOURAGE EACH OTHER,

LISTEN TO EACH OTHER,

LEARN FROM EACH OTHER,

SPEAK TRUTH TO EACH OTHER,

FORGIVE EACH OTHER,

AND LOVE EACH OTHER.

AMEN.

THANK YOU, LORD JESUS,
FOR YOUR WORD,
WHICH INSTRUCTS ME
TO LIVE A LIFE OF WISDOM
AND THOUGHTFULNESS
AND REAL JOY.
AMEN.

———

NEVER STOP PRAYING.

—1 THESSALONIANS 5:17 NLT

DEAR GOD,

AS I JOIN WITH YOU IN PRAYER,

I AM ONE WITH MY CREATOR.

I KNOW THE PEACE OF GOD,

THE PEACE THAT PASSES

ALL UNDERSTANDING.

THANK YOU FOR THE GIFT OF PEACE.

· · · · · · · · · ·  · · · · · · · · · ·

PRAYER IS NOTHING ELSE

THAN BEING ON TERMS

OF FRIENDSHIP WITH GOD.

—SAINT TERESA OF AVILA

FATHER GOD,
MY MIND IS TROUBLED
AND CONFUSED.
I WANT TO REST
IN YOUR ARMS.
I WANT TO TURN ALL
OF MY THOUGHTS
TO YOU.
AMEN.

NOW IS YOUR TIME OF GRIEF,

BUT I WILL SEE YOU AGAIN

AND YOU WILL REJOICE,

AND NO ONE WILL TAKE AWAY

YOUR JOY.

—JOHN 16:22

O LORD,

MY HEART IS ALL A PRAYER,

BUT IT IS SILENT UNTO THEE;

I AM TOO TIRED

TO LOOK FOR WORDS,

I REST UPON THY SYMPATHY

TO UNDERSTAND WHEN

I AM DUMB,

AND WELL I KNOW

THOU HEAREST ME.

—AMY CARMICHAEL

GUIDE ME IN **YOUR** TRUTH

AND TEACH ME,

FOR YOU ARE **GOD** MY SAVIOR,

AND MY HOPE

IS IN **YOU** ALL DAY LONG.

—PSALM 25:5

DEAR LORD,

"NOT MY WILL BUT

YOURS BE DONE."

I WANT THESE WORDS

TO BE THE ROAD MAP

FOR MY LIFE.

AMEN.

DEAR GOD,
I CONFESS TO YOU MY OWN
UNWORTHINESS AND WEAKNESS,
EVEN AS I HOPE IN YOUR
FAITHFULNESS AND STRENGTH.
THANK YOU FOR ALWAYS BEING
THERE FOR ME, AND HERE FOR ME.
AMEN.

—LILY KENT

SHE SPEAKS WITH WISDOM,
AND FAITHFUL INSTRUCTION
IS ON HER TONGUE.

—PROVERBS 31:26

DEAR JESUS,
TODAY MAY I CHOOSE
LOVE. AMEN.

———

PRAYER IS NOT
ELOQUENCE,
BUT EARNESTNESS.

—HANNAH MORE

ANY CONCERN

TOO SMALL

TO BE TURNED

INTO A PRAYER IS

TOO SMALL

TO BE MADE

INTO A BURDEN.

—CORRIE TEN BOOM

TEACH, LORD,
FOR YOUR SERVANT IS WILLING TO LEARN. AMEN.

I AM CONTENT TO FILL
A LITTLE SPACE
IF GOD BE GLORIFIED.

—SUSANNA WESLEY

TEACH ME, LORD,

TO SING OF YOUR MERCIES.

TURN MY SOUL INTO A GARDEN,

WHERE THE FLOWERS DANCE

IN THE GARDEN BREEZE,

PRAISING YOU

WITH THEIR BEAUTY.

—SAINT TERESA OF AVILA

HOW PRECIOUS ARE YOUR
THOUGHTS ABOUT ME, O GOD.
THEY CANNOT BE NUMBERED!
I CAN'T EVEN COUNT THEM;
THEY OUTNUMBER
THE GRAINS OF SAND!

—PSALM 139:17-18 NLT

CHARM IS DECEPTIVE,

AND BEAUTY IS FLEETING;

BUT A WOMAN WHO FEARS THE LORD

IS TO BE PRAISED.

—PROVERBS 31:30

DEAR LORD,

I ENTRUST TO YOU MY NEEDS,

AS WELL AS THE NEEDS OF THOSE I LOVE.

IN A WORLD WHERE MANY SHADOWS LURK,

MAY YOUR WISDOM AND TRUTH

LIGHT OUR WAY.

AMEN.

PRAYER DOES NOT FIT US FOR GREATER WORK; PRAYER IS THE GREATER WORK.

—OSWALD CHAMBERS

HEAVENLY FATHER,

I INVITE YOU TO ILLUMINATE ME.

I WELCOME YOU WITH

FAITH AND HOPE,

AND I WILL HOLD FIRMLY TO YOUR WORD.

I WILL SHARE THE JOYOUS TRUTH:

JESUS, I BELIEVE IN YOU!

AMEN.

—LILY KENT

ETERNAL GOD,

UNCREATED AND ORIGINAL LIGHT,

MAKER OF ALL CREATED THINGS,

FOUNTAIN OF PITY, SEA OF BOUNTY,

FATHOMLESS DEEP OF LOVING-KINDNESS:

LIFT UP THE LIGHT OF YOUR FACE ON US!

LORD, SHINE IN OUR HEARTS,

TRUE SUN OF RIGHTEOUSNESS,

AND FILL OUR SOULS WITH YOUR BEAUTY.

TEACH US ALWAYS TO REMEMBER

YOUR JUDGMENTS, AND TO SPEAK OF THEM,

AND OWN YOU CONTINUALLY AS

OUR LORD AND FRIEND.

GOVERN THE WORKS OF OUR HANDS

BY YOUR WILL, AND LEAD US IN THE RIGHT WAY,

THAT WE MAY DO WHAT IS PLEASING

AND ACCEPTABLE TO YOU,

THAT THROUGH US UNWORTHY PEOPLE

YOUR HOLY NAME MAY BE GLORIFIED.

TO YOU ALONE BE PRAISE AND HONOR

AND WORSHIP ETERNALLY.

—SAINT BASIL

MY PRAYER FOR TODAY:
MAY TRUE WORDS BE FOUND ON MY LIPS.
MAY I WALK IN PEACE AND INTEGRITY.
MAY I LEAD OTHERS ALONG THE PATH
OF LOVE AND COMPASSION. AMEN.

—INSPIRED BY MALACHI 2:6

PRAY FOR MY SOUL.
MORE THINGS ARE WROUGHT BY PRAYER
THAN THIS WORLD DREAMS OF:
WHEREFORE, LET THY VOICE
RISE LIKE A FOUNTAIN FOR ME
NIGHT AND DAY.

— ALFRED, LORD TENNYSON

HEAVENLY FATHER,

AS I NAVIGATE THE DAY AHEAD,

MAY I GIVE CAREFUL THOUGHT

TO MY WAYS. AMEN.

—INSPIRED BY HAGGAI 1:7

———

PRAYER IS THE
EASIEST AND HARDEST
OF ALL THINGS.

—E.M. BOUNDS

CREATOR GOD,

I THANK YOU THAT I AM ALIVE

BECAUSE YOU GAVE ME BREATH.

AND I THANK YOU FOR DOING THIS

BECAUSE YOU LOVE ME.

AMEN.

—TAYLOR MORGAN

DO NOT GRIEVE,
FOR THE JOY OF
THE LORD IS YOUR
STRENGTH.

— NEHEMIAH 8:10

GIVE ME THE **LOVE** THAT LEADS THE WAY,

THE **FAITH** THAT NOTHING CAN DISMAY,

THE **HOPE** NO DISAPPOINTMENTS TIRE,

THE **PASSION** THAT WILL BURN LIKE FIRE;

LET ME NOT SINK TO BE A CLOD:

MAKE ME THY FUEL, FLAME OF GOD.

—AMY CARMICHAEL

ACT AS IF IT WERE IMPOSSIBLE TO FAIL!

—DOROTHEA BRANDE

COMFORT MY HEART

WHAT WINGS ARE
TO A BIRD AND
SAILS TO A SHIP,
SO IS **PRAYER**
TO THE SOUL.

—CORRIE TEN BOOM

WONDERFUL GOD OF ALL COMFORT,

STEADY ME, SUSTAIN ME, STRENGTHEN ME, SURROUND ME

WITH YOUR SPIRIT. AMEN.

—PAT LAWRENCE

ABOVE ALL ELSE, GUARD YOUR HEART,
FOR EVERYTHING YOU DO FLOWS FROM IT.

—PROVERBS 4:23

DEAR GOD,

WHEN LIFE PUSHES ME TOWARD
YET ANOTHER STORM,
PLEASE PULL ME BACK
INTO YOUR PEACE.
AMEN.

———

WHAT WE **CHOOSE** TO USE
AS OUR ANCHOR
DETERMINES HOW WELL
WE WILL WEATHER
THE SEASONS OF LIFE.

—LAUREN CHANDLER

LORD,

THANK YOU FOR ASSURING ME
THAT MY CURRENT PREDICAMENT
IS NOT MY FINAL DESTINATION.

THE PRAYER OF A
RIGHTEOUS PERSON
IS POWERFUL
AND EFFECTIVE.

—JAMES 5:16

MAY YOUR
TROUBLES BE LESS
AND YOUR
BLESSINGS BE MORE,
AND NOTHING BUT HAPPINESS
COME THROUGH YOUR DOOR.

—THOMAS MERTON

THE LORD IS CLOSE
TO THE BROKENHEARTED,
AND HE SAVES THOSE
WHOSE SPIRITS
HAVE BEEN CRUSHED.

—PSALM 34:18 NCV

O KING OF **NIGHT** AND **DAY,**
MORE SAFE AM I WITHIN THY HAND
THAN IF A HOST DID ROUND ME STAND.

—SAINT COLUMBA

TAKE THE VERY HARDEST THING
IN YOUR LIFE—
THE PLACE OF DIFFICULTY,
OUTWARD OR INWARD,
AND EXPECT GOD TO TRIUMPH
GLORIOUSLY IN THAT VERY SPOT.
JUST THERE HE CAN BRING
YOUR SOUL INTO BLOSSOM.

—LILIAS TROTTER

A PRAYER OF PROTECTION

THE LIGHT OF GOD SURROUNDS ME;

THE LOVE OF GOD ENFOLDS ME;

THE POWER OF GOD PROTECTS ME;

THE PRESENCE OF GOD WATCHES OVER ME.

WHEREVER I AM, GOD IS.

—JAMES DILLET FREEMAN

HEAVENLY FATHER,
PLEASE BRING PEACE TO MY HEART
SO THAT I CAN SHARE PEACE WITH OTHERS.
AMEN.

IF THE HEART WANDERS OR IS DISTRACTED,

BRING IT BACK TO THE POINT QUITE GENTLY

AND REPLACE IT TENDERLY IN
ITS MASTER'S PRESENCE.

AND EVEN IF YOU DID NOTHING
DURING THE WHOLE

OF YOUR HOUR BUT BRING YOUR HEART BACK

AND PLACE IT AGAIN IN OUR LORD'S PRESENCE,

THOUGH IT WENT AWAY EVERY
TIME YOU BROUGHT IT BACK,

YOUR HOUR WILL BE VERY WELL EMPLOYED.

—SAINT FRANCIS DE SALES

ABIDE IN ME, O LORD, AND I IN THEE;
FROM THIS GOOD HOUR,
O LEAVE ME NEVERMORE;
THEN SHALL THE DISCORD CEASE,
THE WOUND BE HEALED,
THE LIFE-LONG BLEEDING
OF THE SOUL BE O'ER.

—HARRIET BEECHER STOWE

IN PRAYER, THE DISTANCE
BETWEEN HUMANKIND
AND GOD CAN BE BRIDGED.

—TAYLOR MORGAN

LOOK UPON US, O LORD,

AND LET THE DARKNESS

OF OUR SOULS

VANISH BEFORE THE BEAMS

OF THY BRIGHTNESS.

FILL US WITH HOLY LOVE,

AND OPEN TO US THE TREASURES

OF THY WISDOM.

ALL OUR DESIRE IS KNOWN

UNTO THEE;

THEREFORE PERFECT WHAT

THOU HAST BEGUN,

AND WHAT THY SPIRIT HAS

AWAKENED US TO ASK IN PRAYER.

WE SEEK THY FACE;

TURN THY FACE UNTO US

AND SHOW US THY GLORY.

THEN SHALL OUR LONGING

BE SATISFIED, AND OUR

PEACE SHALL BE PERFECT.

—SAINT AUGUSTINE

HOLD ON, DEAR FRIEND,

FOR THIS IS NOT THE END.

YOU HAVE TRAVELED SO FAR,

AND YOU HAVE WORKED SO HARD.

CARRY ON WITH COURAGE

AND DO NOT GIVE UP.

AND NOT BECAUSE THINGS WILL BE EASY,

BUT BECAUSE THESE SEEDS

YOU ARE SOWING MATTER,

AND THEY WILL GROW IN TIME,

IF YOU DO NOT LOSE HEART.

—MORGAN HARPER NICHOLS

BE GRACIOUS TO OUR NECESSITIES,
AND GUARD US, AND ALL WE LOVE,
FROM EVIL THIS NIGHT.

—JANE AUSTEN

GIVE ME THE **COURAGE**
TO STAND THE PAIN
TO GET THE GRACE, O LORD.

—FLANNERY O'CONNOR

I LOVE YOU, LORD.

YOU ARE MY STRENGTH.

YOU ARE MY ROCK,
MY PROTECTION,
MY SAVIOR.

I CAN RUN TO YOU FOR SAFETY.

YOU ARE MY SHIELD,

MY SAVING STRENGTH,

AND MY DEFENDER.

—INSPIRED BY PSALM 18:2

O HOPE, DAZZLING,
RADIANT HOPE—

WHAT A CHANGE THOU
BRINGEST TO THE HOPELESS,

BRIGHTENING THE
DARKENED PATHS,

AND CHEERING
THE LONELY WAY.

—AIMEE SEMPLE McPHERSON

EVEN IF I HAD ALL
THE CRIMES POSSIBLE
ON MY CONSCIENCE,
I AM SURE I SHOULD LOSE
NONE OF MY CONFIDENCE.
HEARTBROKEN WITH REPENTANCE,
I WOULD SIMPLY THROW MYSELF
INTO MY SAVIOR'S ARMS,
FOR I KNOW HOW MUCH HE LOVES
THE PRODIGAL SON.

—SAINT THERESE OF LISIEUX

THANK YOU,
LORD, FOR ALWAYS . . .
CLEARING MY MIND,
HEALING MY HEART,
AND RESTORING MY SOUL.
AMEN.

———

IT'S COMPLETELY
THROUGH PRAYER
THAT I CAME
TO BELIEVE IN GOD.

—MARY KARR

GOD WHO CARRIES US

IN HIS ARMS,

SAILING ON SEAS

CALM AND STORMY,

HEAR OUR PRAYERS....

I BIND UNTO MYSELF THIS DAY

THE STRONG NAME

OF THE TRINITY.

—TRADITIONAL CELTIC LITURGY

O LORD,

DON'T PASS

ME BY.

—FANNY CROSBY

I FELT THE LORD WOULD GIVE ME

THE STRENGTH

TO ENDURE WHATEVER I HAD TO FACE.

GOD DID AWAY WITH ALL MY FEAR. . .

IT WAS TIME FOR SOMEONE TO STAND UP—

OR, IN MY CASE, SIT DOWN.

I REFUSED TO MOVE.

—ROSA PARKS

JESUS, IN YOU ALONE
MY MIND FINDS PEACE,
MY BODY FINDS COMFORT,
MY SOUL FINDS REST.
AMEN.

IN SPITE OF EVERYTHING,
I FEEL THAT I AM FILLED WITH COURAGE;
I AM SURE THAT GOD IS NOT
GOING TO ABANDON ME.
OH, I WANT TO REFUSE HIM NOTHING,
AND EVEN THOUGH I FEEL SAD
AND ALONE ON THIS EARTH,
HE STILL REMAINS WITH ME.

—SAINT THERESE OF LISIEUX

DEAR GOD,

PLEASE REVEAL TO US YOUR

SUBLIME BEAUTY THAT IS

EVERYWHERE,

EVERYWHERE,

EVERYWHERE,

SO THAT WE WILL NEVER AGAIN

FEEL FRIGHTENED.

MY DIVINE LOVE, MY LOVE,

PLEASE LET US TOUCH YOUR FACE.

—SAINT FRANCIS OF ASSISI

GOVERN EVERYTHING BY YOUR WISDOM, O LORD,

SO THAT MY SOUL
MAY ALWAYS BE SERVING YOU

IN THE WAY YOU WILL
AND NOT AS I CHOOSE.

LET ME DIE TO MYSELF
SO THAT I MAY SERVE YOU;

LET ME LIVE TO YOU,
WHO ARE LIFE ITSELF.

AMEN.

—SAINT TERESA OF AVILA

HEAVENLY FATHER,

PLEASE KEEP MY HEART PURE.

AMEN.

—————

BE THE REASON
SOMEONE BELIEVES
IN THE GOODNESS
OF PEOPLE.

—KAREN SALMANSOHN

MERCIFUL GOD,
HELP ME TO ACCEPT
THAT THE PEOPLE
WHO ARE HARDEST
FOR ME TO LOVE
ARE OFTEN THE ONES
WHO NEED MY LOVE
THE MOST.

I WILL SAY OF THE LORD,
"HE IS MY REFUGE
AND MY FORTRESS,
MY GOD, IN WHOM I TRUST."

—PSALM 91:2

LOVING FATHER,

YOU KNOW MY TROUBLES
BETTER THAN ANYONE.

YOU COMFORT ME
WHEN OTHERS ABANDON ME.

YOU REMEMBER MY NAME
AND SEARCH FOR ME

IN MY DARKEST HOURS.

I REMEMBER YOU, TOO,

AND I TURN TO YOU NOW.

I HEAR YOUR VOICE,

AND I RUN DESPERATELY TO YOU.

HELP ME, PLEASE.

AMEN.

—LILY KENT

I DO NOT KNOW, O GOD,

WHAT WILL HAPPEN TO ME TODAY,

I KNOW ONLY THAT NOTHING

WILL HAPPEN TO ME

BUT WHAT HAS BEEN FORESEEN BY YOU

FROM ALL ETERNITY,

AND THAT IS SUFFICIENT,

O MY GOD, TO KEEP ME IN PEACE.

I ADORE YOUR ETERNAL DESIGNS.

I SUBMIT TO THEM WITH

ALL MY HEART.

—ELISABETH OF FRANCE

DEAR JESUS,
MAY I FACE TODAY
WITH AN
OPEN HEART,
NOT A CLOSED MIND.
AMEN.

❦

I HAVE BEEN DRIVEN MANY TIMES

UPON MY KNEES BY THE OVERWHELMING

CONVICTION THAT I HAD NOWHERE ELSE TO GO.

MY OWN WISDOM AND THAT OF ALL ABOUT ME

SEEMED INSUFFICIENT FOR THAT DAY.

—ABRAHAM LINCOLN

LORD JESUS,

YOU ARE A SHIELD AROUND ME.

STRONG IN LOVE,

HEAVY WITH POWER.

SHAPED WITH HOPE AND

GILDED WITH TRUTH.

I WILL FEAR NO EVIL,

FOR YOU WATCH OVER ME.

IN THIS DAY,

THIS HOUR,

THIS MOMENT,

I PUT MY TRUST IN YOU.

—INSPIRED BY PSALM 3

NOW TO HIM WHO IS ABLE TO DO
IMMEASURABLY MORE
THAN ALL WE ASK OR IMAGINE,
ACCORDING TO HIS POWER
THAT IS AT WORK WITHIN US,
TO HIM BE GLORY IN THE CHURCH
AND IN CHRIST JESUS
THROUGHOUT ALL GENERATIONS,
FOR EVER AND EVER! AMEN.

—EPHESIANS 3:20-21

IF YOU WOKE UP BREATHING,
CONGRATULATIONS!
YOU HAVE ANOTHER CHANCE.

—ANDREA BOYDSTON

A PRAYER OF BLESSING

LORD, PLEASE BLESS US AS WE REST,

RESTORE US AS WE SLEEP.

YOU CARE FOR US AS WE DRIFT OFF,

AND MAKE OUR DREAMING SWEET.

— ANONYMOUS

❧

THEY ALL JOINED TOGETHER

CONSTANTLY IN PRAYER,

ALONG WITH THE WOMEN

AND MARY THE MOTHER OF JESUS,

AND WITH HIS BROTHERS.

— ACTS 1:14

MY HEART'S PRAYER TODAY, LORD,

IS THAT I MAY DISCOVER BEAUTY,

MEANING, AND FULFILLMENT,

ESPECIALLY WHEN THINGS

DON'T TURN OUT AS I HOPE THEY WILL.

IN JESUS'S NAME.

CALL FOR HELP
WHEN YOU'RE IN TROUBLE—
I'LL HELP YOU,
AND YOU'LL HONOR ME.

—PSALM 50:15 MSG

O LORD MY GOD,

TEACH MY HEART THIS DAY
WHERE AND HOW TO SEE YOU,
WHERE AND HOW TO FIND YOU.
YOU HAVE MADE ME AND REMADE ME,
AND YOU HAVE BESTOWED ON ME
ALL THE GOOD THINGS I POSSESS,
AND STILL I DO NOT KNOW YOU.
I HAVE NOT YET DONE THAT
FOR WHICH I WAS MADE.
TEACH ME TO SEEK YOU,
FOR I CANNOT SEEK YOU
UNLESS YOU TEACH ME, OR FIND YOU
UNLESS YOU SHOW YOURSELF TO ME.
LET ME SEEK YOU IN MY DESIRE,
LET ME DESIRE YOU IN MY SEEKING.
LET ME FIND YOU BY LOVING YOU,
LET ME LOVE YOU WHEN I FIND YOU.

—SAINT ANSELM

MAY GOD THE FATHER
BLESS US,

MAY CHRIST
TAKE CARE OF US,

THE HOLY GHOST
ENLIGHTEN US

ALL THE DAYS OF OUR LIFE.
THE LORD BE OUR DEFENDER
AND KEEPER OF BODY AND SOUL,
BOTH NOW AND FOREVER,
TO THE AGES OF AGES.

—SAINT ÆTHELWOLD

MY HEART REJOICES IN THE LORD;
IN THE LORD MY HORN IS LIFTED HIGH.
MY MOUTH BOASTS OVER MY ENEMIES,
FOR I DELIGHT IN YOUR DELIVERANCE.

—HANNAH, MOTHER OF SAMUEL
1 SAMUEL 2:1

PRAYER IS THE CONTACT
OF A LIVING SOUL WITH GOD.
IN PRAYER, GOD STOOPS TO KISS MAN,
TO BLESS MAN, AND TO AID IN
EVERYTHING THAT GOD CAN DEVISE
OR MAN CAN NEED.

—E.M. BOUNDS

FORWARD

I GO WITH YOU, LORD,

THE ONE WHO HOLDS MY HEART.

ONE STEP **AT A TIME,**

ONE BREATH **AT A TIME,**

ONE MOMENT **AT A TIME.**

AMEN.

A BLESSING FOR YOU

MAY YOU LIVE A LIFE WORTHY OF OUR LORD.

MAY YOU PLEASE HIM EVERY DAY,

AS YOU DO GOOD THINGS AND LEARN
  MORE AND MORE

ABOUT GOD AND HIS AMAZING SON.

MAY HE GIVE YOU STRENGTH AND ENDURANCE.

MAY YOU GIVE JOYFUL THANKS ALWAYS TO THE ONE

WHO HAS LET YOU ENTER THE KINGDOM OF LIGHT.

—INSPIRED BY COLOSSIANS 1:10-12

———

HE IS THE ONE YOU PRAISE;

HE IS YOUR GOD,

WHO PERFORMED FOR YOU

THOSE GREAT AND AWESOME WONDERS

YOU SAW WITH YOUR OWN EYES.

—DEUTERONOMY 10:21

MY HEART REJOICES
EVEN IN TROUBLE,
BECAUSE YOU, MY GOD,
ARE SO MUCH BIGGER
THAN MY PROBLEMS.
AMEN.

DO NOT BE DISMAYED BY THE
BROKENNESS OF THE WORLD.
ALL THINGS BREAK.
AND ALL THINGS CAN BE MENDED.
NOT WITH TIME . . .
BUT WITH INTENTION. SO GO.
LOVE INTENTIONALLY, EXTRAVAGANTLY,
UNCONDITIONALLY.
THE BROKEN WORLD
WAITS IN THE DARKNESS
FOR THE LIGHT THAT IS YOU.

—L.R. KNOST

MAY ALL YOUR
ENEMIES PERISH, LORD!
BUT MAY ALL WHO
LOVE YOU
BE LIKE THE SUN
WHEN IT RISES
IN ITS STRENGTH.

—DEBORAH, ISRAEL'S ONLY FEMALE JUDGE
JUDGES 5:31

EMPOWER
MY LIFE

WHATEVER MY **CHALLENGES** MIGHT BE TODAY, I BELIEVE THEY ARE HELPLESS AGAINST MY **PRAYERS.**

—LILY KENT

O HEAVENLY FATHER,

I PRAISE AND THANK YOU

FOR REST IN THE NIGHT;

I PRAISE AND THANK YOU

FOR THIS NEW DAY;

I PRAISE AND THANK YOU

FOR ALL YOUR GOODNESS

AND FAITHFULNESS

THROUGHOUT MY LIFE.

—DIETRICH BONHOEFFER

I AM THE LORD'S SERVANT.
MAY EVERYTHING YOU HAVE SAID
ABOUT ME COME TRUE.

—MARY, MOTHER OF JESUS
LUKE 1:38 NLT

THE MORE PRAYING
THERE IS IN THE WORLD,
THE BETTER THE WORLD
WILL BE.

—E.M. BOUNDS

THE WORLD FOR GOD!
THE WORLD FOR GOD!

THERE'S NOTHING ELSE WILL MEET

THE HUNGER OF MY SOUL.

—EVANGELINE CORY BOOTH

SING TO THE LORD,
FOR HE HAS TRIUMPHED GLORIOUSLY;
THE HORSE AND HIS RIDER HE HAS
THROWN INTO THE SEA.

—MIRIAM, THE SISTER OF MOSES
EXODUS 15:21 ESV

EACH TIME,

BEFORE YOU INTERCEDE,

BE QUIET FIRST,

**AND WORSHIP GOD
IN HIS GLORY.**

THINK OF WHAT HE CAN DO,

AND HOW HE DELIGHTS

TO HEAR THE PRAYERS

OF HIS REDEEMED PEOPLE.

—CHRISTINA ROSSETTI

HEAVENLY FATHER,
I PRAISE YOU
BECAUSE YOUR LOVE FOR ME
IS MIGHTIER THAN
THE WAVES OF THE SEA.

—INSPIRED BY PSALM 93:4

LIFT UP YOUR HEADS, YE PEOPLE,
LIFT UP YOUR FACES, TOO;
OPEN YOUR MOUTHS TO SING HIS PRAISE,
AND THE RAIN WILL FALL ON YOU.

—AIMEE SEMPLE MCPHERSON

OPEN WIDE

THE WINDOW OF OUR SPIRITS,

O LORD, AND FILL US FULL OF LIGHT;

OPEN WIDE

THE DOOR OF OUR HEARTS,

THAT WE MAY RECEIVE

AND ENTERTAIN THEE

WITH ALL OUR POWERS

OF ADORATION AND LOVE.

—CHRISTINA ROSSETTI

GLORY BE TO THE FATHER,

AND TO THE SON,

AND TO THE HOLY GHOST.

AS IT WAS

IN THE BEGINNING,

IS NOW,

AND EVER SHALL BE,

WORLD WITHOUT END.

AMEN.

MAY THE **COMFORTS** OF EVERY DAY
BE **THANKFULLY** FELT BY US,
MAY THEY PROMPT A WILLING OBEDIENCE
OF THY COMMANDMENTS
AND A BENEVOLENT SPIRIT
TOWARD **EVERY** FELLOW-CREATURE.

—JANE AUSTEN

READ MY LETTER TO THE OLD FOLKS,
AND GIVE MY LOVE TO THEM,
AND TELL MY BROTHERS TO ALWAYS BE
WATCHING UNTO PRAYER,
AND WHEN THE GOOD OLD SHIP OF ZION
COMES ALONG, TO BE READY TO STEP ABOARD.

—HARRIET TUBMAN

HEAVENLY FATHER,

WHEN IT SEEMS YOU ARE SILENT,
HELP ME TO REMEMBER THAT SILENCE
IS NOT NECESSARILY EMPTY.

**SILENCE CAN BE FULL OF INSIGHT,
CLARITY, AND PEACE.**

I THANK YOU FOR THE BLESSING
OF SILENCE. AMEN.

—PAT LAWRENCE

ALL PRAISE TO THE GOD AND
FATHER OF OUR LORD JESUS CHRIST!

ACCORDING TO HIS ABUNDANT MERCY;

HE HAS FILLED US WITH LIFE AND HOPE

BY THE RESURRECTION OF JESUS CHRIST
FROM THE DEAD.

OUR HOLY INHERITANCE IS PURE AND
INCORRUPTIBLE.

IT WILL NEVER FADE AWAY; IT IS RESERVED
IN HEAVEN FOR US.

SAVE US, FATHER, BY YOUR POWER;
ENCOURAGE US BY YOUR GIFT OF FAITH.

THAT FAITH, MORE PRECIOUS THAN GOLD,
WILL ENDURE,

EVEN THOUGH IT MAY BE TESTED WITH FIRE.

IT WILL SHINE WITH HONOR AND GLORY

AT THE APPEARING OF OUR SAVIOR,
JESUS CHRIST.

AMEN.

—INSPIRED BY 1 PETER 1:3-7

MY LONGING FOR TRUTH WAS A

SINGLE PRAYER.

LORD JESUS,

TODAY MAY I DISCOVER THE FREEDOM

OF NOT OBSESSING OVER

WHAT OTHER PEOPLE THINK.

AMEN.

MERCIFUL GOD,

I AM SO GRATEFUL THAT YOUR GRACE
IS ALWAYS BIGGER THAN MY SIN.

AMEN.

TO GIVE THANKS
IN SOLITUDE IS ENOUGH.
THANKSGIVING HAS WINGS
AND GOES WHERE IT MUST GO.
YOUR PRAYER
KNOWS MUCH MORE
ABOUT IT THAN YOU DO.

—VICTOR HUGO

MÜDE BIN ICH, GEH' ZUR RUH
(WEARY NOW, I GO TO REST)

WEARY NOW, I GO TO REST,
CLOSE MY EYES IN SLUMBER BLEST.
FATHER, MAY THY WATCHFUL EYE
GUARD THE BED ON WHICH I LIE.

WRONG I MAY HAVE DONE TODAY,
HEED IT NOT, DEAR GOD, I PRAY.
FOR THY MERCY AND CHRIST SLAIN
TURNS ALL WRONG TO RIGHT AGAIN.

MAY MY LOVED ONES, SAFE FROM HARM,
REST WITHIN THY SHELTERING ARM.
ALL THY CHILDREN EVERYWHERE
SHALL FIND REFUGE IN THY CARE.

SEND THY **REST** TO HEARTS IN PAIN,
CLOSE THE WEARY EYES AGAIN.
GOD IN HEAVEN THY VIGIL KEEP;
GRANT US ALL A **RESTFUL** SLEEP.

AMEN.

—LUISE HENSEL

(This prayer, written by poet and hymn writer Luise Hensel, first appeared
in a German songbook for nursery-school children in 1842. The rendering
above is one of several English translations.)

I THANK YOU, GOD,
FOR CREATING ME

TO MANIFEST YOUR
GLORY WITHIN ME.

AS I LET YOUR
LIGHT SHINE,

MAY I INSPIRE OTHERS
TO DO THE SAME.

AMEN.

PRAYER
LINKS SOULS TOGETHER.

—SAINT ELIZABETH OF THE TRINITY

———

LOVING LORD AND HEAVENLY FATHER,
I OFFER UP TODAY
    ALL THAT I AM,
    ALL THAT I HAVE,
    ALL THAT I DO, AND
    ALL THAT I SUFFER,
TO BE YOURS TODAY AND YOURS FOREVER.
GIVE ME GRACE, LORD, TO DO
    ALL THAT I KNOW
OF YOUR HOLY WILL.

—ELISABETH ELLIOT

GIVE ME A PURE, FRESH HEART

THAT IS NOT DESPONDENT,

SO THAT I MAY

WORSHIP YOU

WITH ALL MY HEART,

AND WITHOUT FALSEHOOD,

NOT GRUDGINGLY OR SADLY,

BUT GLADLY AND JOYFULLY,

SO THAT I MAY CARRY OUT

YOUR COMMANDMENTS

WITH GREAT HAPPINESS. . . .

—RIVKE TIKTINER

BELOVED GOD,
CREATOR OF ALL SOULS,

I PRAISE YOU AND THANK YOU,

FOR CHOOSING US
AS YOUR BELOVED PEOPLE.

YOU ARE OUR GOD,
WHO CREATED HEAVEN
AND EARTH....

MAY WE BE WORTHY TO BE IN
THIS WORLD, AND IN THE NEXT.

AMEN.

LORD OF THE FIELD,

LORD OF THE WIND,

CHRIST JESUS,

INTERCESSOR,

TEACH US TO PRAY.

—AMY CARMICHAEL

THE LORD SAID TO HIM:

"I HAVE HEARD THE PRAYER AND THE PLEA

YOU HAVE MADE BEFORE ME."

—1 KINGS 9:3

DEAR LORD,

I WOKE UP TODAY.

I HAVE CLOTHES.

I HAVE FOOD.

I CAN READ.

I CAN PRAY.

I CAN LOVE.

I AM THANKFUL.

AND I AM YOURS!

—VICTORIA RAY

SETTLE MY SILLY HEART,
GOOD LORD.

HOLD ME STILL
IN YOUR MOTHERLY EMBRACE,

ENFOLDED BY YOUR WINGS
OF PEACE AND LOVE,

AND TOTAL ACCEPTANCE.
SOOTHE ME, LOVE ME
INTO PEACE.

—DOROTHY STEWART

PLEASE HELP ME, FATHER,

TO PROTECT MY COMMUNITY,

CARE FOR THE POOR, FORGIVE TIRELESSLY,

AND FIGHT FOR THE POWERLESS.

MAY I SHARE MY RESOURCES,

BOTH THE SPIRITUAL AND THE PHYSICAL.

MAY I EMBRACE THE OUTCAST, AS JESUS DID.

MAY I LOVE MY GOD,

AND CHERISH THE LIFE I HAVE BEEN GIVEN.

AMEN.

—PAT LAWRENCE

TEACH US, ALMIGHTY FATHER,

TO CONSIDER THIS SOLEMN TRUTH,

AS WE SHOULD DO,

THAT WE MAY FEEL THE IMPORTANCE OF

EVERY DAY, AND EVERY HOUR

AS IT PASSES, AND EARNESTLY STRIVE

TO MAKE A BETTER USE OF WHAT

THY GOODNESS MAY YET BESTOW ON US,

THAN WE HAVE DONE OF THE TIME PAST.

—JANE AUSTEN

I MAKE A **SACRIFICE**

OF EVERYTHING.

I UNITE THIS **SACRIFICE**

TO THAT OF YOUR DEAR SON,

MY SAVIOR,

BEGGING YOU BY HIS INFINITE MERITS,

FOR THE PATIENCE IN TROUBLES,

AND THE PERFECT SUBMISSION

WHICH IS DUE TO YOU IN ALL

THAT YOU WILL AND DESIGN FOR ME.

—ELISABETH OF FRANCE

FOR THE CHILDREN IN MY LIFE

THANK YOU, GOD, FOR THE GIFT

OF **CHILDREN** IN MY LIFE.

HELP ME TO SHOW THEM

YOUR LOVE AND GRACE.

I WANT TO TEACH THEM

THE **BEST** WAY TO LIVE,

SO THAT AS THEY LEARN AND GROW,

THEY WILL **FOLLOW** YOU

EVER MORE CLOSELY.

—LILY KENT

GIVE, I PRAY THEE,

TO ALL CHILDREN GRACE

REVERENTLY TO LOVE THEIR PARENTS,

AND LOVINGLY OBEY THEM.

TEACH US THAT FILIAL DUTY

NEVER ENDS OR LESSENS;

AND BLESS ALL PARENTS IN THEIR CHILDREN,

AND ALL CHILDREN IN THEIR PARENTS.

— CHRISTINA ROSSETTI

FATHER GOD,
I PLACE

MY LIFE IN
YOUR HANDS,

BECAUSE
I WANT TO SEE

YOUR HAND
IN MY LIFE.

AMEN.

THERE IS **NO ONE** HOLY LIKE THE LORD;
THERE IS **NO ONE** BESIDES YOU;
THERE IS **NO ROCK** LIKE OUR GOD.

—HANNAH, MOTHER OF SAMUEL
1 SAMUEL 2:2

PRAYER AND PAINS,
THROUGH FAITH IN CHRIST JESUS,
WILL DO **ANYTHING.**

—MARY ANN EVANS
(ALSO KNOWN AS GEORGE ELIOT)

LORD OF MY DARKEST PLACE:
LET IN YOUR **LIGHT.**

LORD OF MY GREATEST FEAR:
LET IN YOUR **PEACE.**

LORD OF MY MOST BITTER SHAME:
LET IN YOUR **GRACE.**

LORD OF MY OLDEST GRUDGE:
LET IN YOUR **FORGIVENESS.**

LORD OF MY DEEPEST ANGER:
LET **IT OUT.**

LORD OF MY LONELIEST MOMENT:
LET IN YOUR **PRESENCE.**

LORD OF MY TRUEST SELF—MY ALL:
LET IN YOUR **FULLNESS.**

—ALISON PEPPER

BLESSED BE YOU,

MY GOD,

FOR HAVING CREATED ME.

—SAINT CLARE OF ASSISI

GOD SHAPES THE WORLD BY

PRAYER.

—MOTHER TERESA

GOOD, GOOD FATHER,
REASSURE ME TODAY THAT
LOVE IS NOT WHAT I SAY;
LOVE IS WHAT I DO.
IN JESUS'S NAME,
AMEN.

❧

LET US HAVE FAITH
THAT RIGHT MAKES MIGHT,
AND IN THAT FAITH,
LET US, TO THE END,
DARE TO DO OUR DUTY
AS WE UNDERSTAND IT.

—ABRAHAM LINCOLN

MY PRAYER

COURAGE AND PATIENCE, THESE I ASK;
    DEAR LORD, IN THIS MY LATEST STRAIT;
    FOR HARD I FIND MY TEN YEARS' TASK,
    LEARNING TO SUFFER AND TO WAIT.

LIFE SEEMS SO RICH AND GRAND A THING,
    SO FULL OF WORK FOR HEART AND BRAIN,
    IT IS A CROSS THAT I CAN BRING
    NO HELP, NO OFFERING, BUT PAIN.

THE HARD-EARNED HARVEST OF THESE YEARS
    I LONG TO GENEROUSLY SHARE;
    THE LESSONS LEARNED WITH BITTER TEARS
    TO TEACH AGAIN WITH TENDER CARE;

TO SMOOTH THE ROUGH AND THORNY WAY

    WHERE OTHER FEET BEGIN TO TREAD;

    TO FEED SOME HUNGRY SOUL EACH DAY

    WITH SYMPATHY'S SUSTAINING BREAD.

SO BEAUTIFUL SUCH PLEASURES SHOW,

    I LONG TO MAKE THEM MINE;

    TO LOVE AND LABOR AND TO KNOW

    THE JOY SUCH LIVING MAKES DIVINE.

BUT IF I MAY NOT, I WILL ONLY ASK

    COURAGE AND PATIENCE FOR MY FATE,

    AND LEARN, DEAR LORD, THY LATEST TASK,

    TO SUFFER PATIENTLY AND WAIT.

—LOUISA MAY ALCOTT

FIRST, KEEP **PEACE**
WITHIN YOURSELF;
THEN YOU CAN ALSO BRING
PEACE TO OTHERS.

—THOMAS À KEMPIS

———

SLOW ME DOWN, LORD.
EASE THE POUNDING OF MY HEART
BY THE QUIETING OF MY MIND.
STEADY MY HARRIED PACE
WITH A VISION OF THE
ETERNAL REACH OF TIME.

—WILFERD PETERSON

MAKE US WORTHY, LORD,

TO SERVE OUR FELLOW MEN

THROUGHOUT THE WORLD

WHO LIVE AND DIE

IN POVERTY AND HUNGER.

GIVE THEM THROUGH OUR HANDS

THIS DAY THEIR DAILY BREAD,

AND BY OUR UNDERSTANDING LOVE,

GIVE PEACE AND JOY.

—MOTHER TERESA

GOD TO ENFOLD ME,

GOD TO SURROUND ME,

GOD IN MY SPEAKING,

GOD IN MY THINKING,

GOD IN MY SLEEPING,

GOD IN MY WAKING,

GOD IN MY WATCHING,

GOD IN MY HOPING.

GOD IN MY LIFE,

GOD IN MY LIPS,

GOD IN MY SOUL,

GOD IN MY HEART,

GOD IN MY SUFFICING,

GOD IN MY SLUMBER,

GOD IN MY EVER-LIVING SOUL,

GOD IN MY ETERNITY.

—ANCIENT CELTIC BLESSING

OPEN OUR HEARTS TO THE CRIES

OF A SUFFERING WORLD

AND THE HEALING MELODIES OF **PEACE**

AND **JUSTICE** FOR ALL CREATION.

EMPOWER US TO BE INSTRUMENTS OF JUSTICE.

—JEAN S. BOLEN

DEAR GOD,

IF I ERR TODAY,

MAY I ERR ON THE SIDE OF

LOVE AND MERCY.

AMEN.

I AM LEAVING YOU WITH A GIFT—

PEACE OF MIND AND HEART.

AND THE PEACE I GIVE IS A GIFT

THE WORLD CANNOT GIVE.

SO DON'T BE TROUBLED OR AFRAID.

—JOHN 14:27 NLT

RESTORE
MY SOUL

THE LORD IS MY SHEPHERD,
I LACK NOTHING.
HE MAKES ME LIE DOWN
IN GREEN PASTURES.
HE LEADS ME BESIDE
QUIET WATERS,
HE REFRESHES MY SOUL.
HE GUIDES ME ALONG
THE RIGHT PATHS
FOR HIS NAME'S SAKE.

—PSALM 23:1-3

LORD, YOU ARE

MY LOVE, MY LONGING,

MY FLOWING STREAM, MY SUN,

AND I AM YOUR REFLECTION.

—MECHTHILD OF MAGDEBURG

I AM WORKING TOWARD A WORLD

IN WHICH IT WOULD BE EASIER

FOR PEOPLE TO BEHAVE DECENTLY.

—DOROTHY DAY

MAY THE SICK AND AFFLICTED
BE NOW, AND EVER,

IN THY CARE;
AND HEARTILY DO WE

PRAY

FOR THE SAFETY OF ALL THAT
TRAVEL BY LAND OR BY SEA,

FOR THE COMFORT AND
PROTECTION OF THE ORPHAN

AND THE WIDOW AND THAT
THY PITY MAY BE SHOWN

UPON ALL CAPTIVES
AND PRISONERS.

—JANE AUSTEN

HOW WONDERFUL, O LORD,

ARE THE WORKS OF YOUR HANDS!

THE HEAVENS DECLARE YOUR GLORY,

THE ARCH OF THE SKY DISPLAYS YOUR HANDIWORK.

THE HEAVENS DECLARE
THE GLORY OF GOD.

IN YOUR LOVE, YOU HAVE GIVEN US THE POWER

TO BEHOLD THE BEAUTY OF YOUR WORLD,

ROBED IN ALL ITS SPLENDOR.

—ANCIENT HEBREW PRAYER

A FAMILY PRAYER

THANK YOU, GOD,
FOR THIS NEW DAY, FOR THE LIFE

YOU ARE GIVING
EACH MEMBER OF MY FAMILY.

BLESS EACH ONE OF US
WITH THE STRENGTH AND HEALTH

WE NEED TO SERVE
YOU TODAY, WITH THE JOY WE NEED.

MAY WE NOT GIVE IN
TO DISCOURAGEMENT, ANGER, OR BOREDOM.

GIVE US THE PROTECTION
WE NEED AGAINST PHYSICAL AND MORAL DANGER,

AND WITH THE LOVE
WE NEED TO GIVE HOPE TO ALL WE MEET.

—AUTHOR UNKNOWN

THE EARTH IS FULL OF YOUR
GOODNESS,

YOUR GREATNESS AND
UNDERSTANDING,

YOUR WISDOM AND
HARMONY.

HOW WONDERFUL ARE
THE LIGHTS THAT YOU
CREATED.

YOU FORMED THEM WITH
STRENGTH AND POWER,

AND THEY SHINE
WONDERFULLY IN THE WORLD,

MAGNIFICENT IN THEIR
SPLENDOR.

THEY ARISE IN RADIANCE
AND GO DOWN IN JOY.

REVERENTLY, THEY FULFILL
YOUR DIVINE WILL.

THEY ARE TRIBUTES TO
YOUR NAME AS THEY EXALT

YOUR SOVEREIGN RULE
IN SONG.

—ANCIENT HYMN

GOD BLESS

THE HONEST AND THE HOLY.

GOD BLESS

THE GOOD AND THE GENEROUS.

GOD BLESS

THE LIGHT-BEARERS AND

THE LOVE-GIVERS.

AMEN.

—TAYLOR MORGAN

TODAY, MAY MY

MIND AND HEART

SEE ALL OF

THE GOOD IN LIFE.

AMEN.

WAGE PEACE
WITH YOUR BREATH.

—JUDYTH HILL

O TEACH ME TO PRAY, LORD.

TEACH ME TO PRAY.

I NEED SOMEONE TO TALK TO,

A FRIEND WHO WILL LISTEN,

I NEED HOPE,

REFRESHMENT.

WHAT WERE THOSE WORDS
I USED TO KNOW?

"YOU WILL FIND A SOLACE THERE."

CAN HE MEAN ME? O PRAISE HIM!

BUT WHAT CAN I SAY?

O TEACH ME TO PRAY, LORD.

TEACH ME TO PRAY.

—JEAN BRYAN

THE FACT THAT
I AM A WOMAN DOES NOT

MAKE ME A DIFFERENT
KIND OF CHRISTIAN,

BUT THE FACT THAT
I AM A CHRISTIAN

MAKES ME A DIFFERENT
KIND OF WOMAN.

— ELISABETH ELLIOT

MY SAVIOR,

I LONG FOR

A FAITH THAT MAKES ME...

STRONG ENOUGH

TO STAND ALONE,

WISE ENOUGH

TO LIVE IN TRUTH, AND

HUMBLE ENOUGH

TO ASK FOR HELP WHEN I NEED IT.

—LILY KENT

GRANT ME GRACE, O MERCIFUL GOD,

TO DESIRE ARDENTLY ALL THAT

IS PLEASING TO YOU,

TO EXAMINE IT PRUDENTLY,

TO ACT IT TRUTHFULLY,

AND TO ACCOMPLISH IT PERFECTLY,

FOR THE PRAISE

AND GLORY OF YOUR NAME.

—SAINT THOMAS AQUINAS

PRAYER

IS NOT OVERCOMING GOD'S RELUCTANCE,

BUT LAYING HOLD OF HIS WILLINGNESS.

—MARTIN LUTHER

LORD, HELP ME TO
LOVE WHAT I HAVE
BEFORE I HAVE TO
MOURN ITS LOSS.

AMEN.

. . . . ❧ . . . .

ALL THINGS FAIL,

BUT THOU, LORD OF ALL,

NEVER FAILEST.

—SAINT TERESA OF AVILA

MAY THE LORD YOUR GOD
LIFT YOU HIGH.

MAY YOU BE BLESSED
IN THE BUSY BIG CITY
OR THE QUIET SMALL TOWN.

MAY GOD BLESS
THE WORK OF YOUR HANDS
AND YOUR BRAIN.

MAY YOU BE BLESSED
IN YOUR HOME, AND FAR, FAR
BEYOND YOUR HOME.

—INSPIRED BY DEUTERONOMY 28:1-12

GENEROUS GOD,

TODAY MAY I COUNT NOT MONEY,

OR CALORIES, OR GRUDGES, OR STEPS.

INSTEAD MAY I COUNT

MY BLESSINGS.

AMEN.

—PAT LAWRENCE

———

LOVE IS THE
GREATEST BEAUTIFIER
IN THE UNIVERSE.

—MAY CHRISTIE

THANK YOU, LORD JESUS,

THAT YOU WILL BE

OUR HIDING PLACE,

WHATEVER HAPPENS.

—CORRIE TEN BOOM

FOR THE EYES OF THE LORD RANGE

THROUGHOUT THE EARTH

TO STRENGTHEN THOSE WHOSE HEARTS

ARE FULLY COMMITTED TO HIM.

—2 CHRONICLES 16:9

DEAR GOD,

HELP ME TO REMEMBER THAT

THE MOST **BEAUTIFUL** WOMAN

IS THE WOMAN WHO SEES

THE **BEAUTY** IN OTHERS.

AMEN.

GOD,
WHAT DO YOU
WANT ME TO NOTICE
RIGHT NOW?

A SINGLE PRAYER
CAN LAUNCH THE JOURNEY
OF A LIFETIME.

—TAYLOR MORGAN

TODAY IS A GIFT
FROM YOU, GOD;
PERHAPS THAT'S WHY
THEY CALL IT
THE PRESENT.
THANK YOU, AND AMEN.

———

I AM NOT AFRAID OF TOMORROW,
FOR I HAVE SEEN YESTERDAY,
AND I LOVE TODAY.

—WILLIAM ALLEN WHITE

THANK YOU, LORD,

FOR REFRESHING MY SOUL.

BECAUSE OF YOU,

MY SPIRIT TAKES FLIGHT.

I AM HOPEFUL AND FREE

TO EXPRESS,

TO EXPLORE,

TO BE WHO YOU

CREATED ME TO BE.

—VICTORIA RAY

DEAR GOD,

AT THE END OF MY LIFE
HERE ON EARTH,

I HOPE THIS CAN BE SAID OF ME:

SHE FOUGHT FOR WHAT WAS
RIGHT AND FAIR;

SHE TOOK RISKS FOR THINGS
THAT MATTERED;

SHE HELPED THOSE IN NEED;

SHE LEFT THE EARTH
A BETTER PLACE,

BECAUSE OF WHAT SHE DID,

BECAUSE OF WHO SHE WAS.

—LILY KENT

WHEN I FEEL LIKE **WORRYING,**

INSTEAD MAY I . . .

SING
SMILE
LEARN
LISTEN
HOPE
LAUGH
WORSHIP
PRAY
LOVE.

AND **LOVE** SOME MORE.

AMEN.

HEAVENLY FATHER,

I AM REALIZING THAT TO MAKE

A DIFFERENCE IN MY WORLD

I MUST DARE TO BE DIFFERENT,

ESPECIALLY WHEN THE TRUTH

NEEDS TO BE SPOKEN,

THE WORK NEEDS TO BE DONE,

AND THE HELP NEEDS TO BE OFFERED.

GIVE ME THE COURAGE, PLEASE,

TO DARE TO BE DIFFERENT.

AMEN.

—PAT LAWRENCE

FATHER GOD,

ENABLE ME TO CHERISH MY YESTERDAYS,

DREAM MY TOMORROWS,

AND LIVE MY TODAYS.

REMIND ME THAT TOMORROW BELONGS

TO THOSE WHO WISELY USE TODAY.

AMEN.

I CAN DO ALL THINGS THROUGH CHRIST WHO STRENGTHENS ME.

—PHILIPPIANS 4:13 NKJV

DEAR GOD,

WHEN I AM CONFUSED,

ASSURE ME THAT LIFE IS

MORE INTERESTING,

MORE INTRIGUING,

AND

MORE CHALLENGING

WHEN YOU DON'T HAVE

ALL THE ANSWERS.

AMEN.

DEEP PEACE
OF THE RUNNING WAVES TO YOU,

DEEP PEACE
OF THE FLOWING AIR TO YOU,

DEEP PEACE
OF THE QUIET EARTH TO YOU,

DEEP PEACE
OF THE SHINING STARS TO YOU.

DEEP PEACE
OF THE SHADES OF NIGHT TO YOU,

MOON AND STARS ALWAYS
GIVING LIGHT TO YOU,

DEEP PEACE
OF CHRIST, THE SON OF PEACE, TO YOU.

—TRADITIONAL GAELIC BLESSING

LORD, SOMEHOW, SOME WAY,
MAKE ME A BLESSING
TO SOMEONE TODAY. AMEN.

———

COME TO ME,
ALL YOU WHO ARE WEARY
AND BURDENED,
AND I WILL GIVE YOU REST.
TAKE MY YOKE UPON YOU
AND LEARN FROM ME,
FOR I AM GENTLE AND
HUMBLE IN HEART,
AND YOU WILL FIND REST
FOR YOUR SOULS.

—MATTHEW 11:28-29

LORD, I THANK YOU FOR THE

SMALL CHALLENGES

OF DAILY LIFE. I KNOW THEY

PREPARE ME FOR THE

GREAT TESTS

OF LIFE. AMEN.

PRAYER IS THE SPIRIT

SPEAKING TRUTH TO TRUTH.

—PHILIP JAMES BAILEY

PURIFY MY HEART,
SANCTIFY MY THINKING,
CORRECT MY DESIRES.
TEACH ME, IN ALL OF TODAY'S
WORK AND TROUBLE
AND JOY, TO RESPOND
WITH HONEST PRAISE,
SIMPLE TRUST, AND
INSTANT OBEDIENCE,
THAT MY LIFE MAY BE IN
TRUTH A LIVING SACRIFICE,
BY THE POWER OF YOUR
HOLY SPIRIT AND IN THE NAME
OF YOUR SON JESUS CHRIST,
MY MASTER AND MY ALL.
AMEN.

—ELISABETH ELLIOT

MAY YOU BE STRENGTHENED
THROUGH HIS GLORIOUS MIGHT

SO THAT YOU CAN ENDURE
EVERYTHING AND HAVE PATIENCE.

MAY YOU GIVE THANKS
WITH JOY TO THE FATHER.

HE HAS ALLOWED YOU TO
TAKE PART IN THE INHERITANCE,

IN THE LIGHT THAT SHINES ON
GOD'S PRECIOUS CHILDREN.

—INSPIRED BY COLOSSIANS 1:11-12

ETERNAL GOD,

AS I ADJUST TO THESE

EVER-CHANGING TIMES,

HELP ME TO HOLD FIRMLY TO

UNCHANGING PRINCIPLES.

AMEN.

O GOD, MAKE CLEAR
TO US EACH ROAD.

O GOD, MAKE SAFE
TO US EACH STEP;

WHEN WE STUMBLE, HOLD US;

WHEN WE FALL, LIFT US UP;

WHEN WE ARE HARD-PRESSED
WITH EVIL, DELIVER US;

AND BRING US AT LAST
TO YOUR GLORY.

—CELTIC PRAYER

I PRAISE YOU, LORD, FOR RESTORING MY SOUL.

DO NOT FEAR,
FOR I AM WITH YOU;

DO NOT BE DISMAYED,
FOR I AM YOUR GOD.

I WILL STRENGTHEN YOU
AND HELP YOU;

I WILL UPHOLD YOU
WITH MY RIGHTEOUS RIGHT HAND.

—ISAIAH 41:10

MY GOD, I AM YOURS FOR
TIME AND ETERNITY.
TEACH ME
TO CAST MYSELF ENTIRELY
INTO THE ARMS OF YOUR
LOVING PROVIDENCE.

—CATHERINE MCAULEY

I AM INCLINED TOWARD GOD,
AND MUST GO THROUGH ALL THINGS
INTO GOD.

—MECHTHILD OF MAGDEBURG

ANGEL OF GOD,

MY GUARDIAN DEAR,

TO WHOM GOD'S LOVE
COMMITS ME HERE,

EVER THIS DAY, BE AT MY SIDE

TO LIGHT AND GUARD,

TO RULE AND GUIDE.

—ANCIENT LITURGICAL PRAYER

LORD GOD, OF MIGHT INCONCEIVABLE,

OF GLORY INCOMPREHENSIBLE,
OF MERCY IMMEASURABLE,

OF BENIGNITY INEFFABLE;
DO THOU, O MASTER,

**LOOK DOWN UPON US
IN THY TENDER LOVE,**

AND SHOW FORTH, TOWARD US
AND THOSE WHO PRAY WITH US,

THY RICH MERCIES AND COMPASSIONS.

AMEN.

—TRADITIONALLY ATTRIBUTED TO
ST. JOHN CHRYSTOSTOM

LORD, BE WITH

EVERY WOMAN WHO IS SICK

AND ENCOURAGE THEM AS ONLY YOU CAN.

I KNOW HOW FAITHFUL YOU ARE.

YOU HAVE SHOWN YOURSELF

TO BE EVERYTHING

YOU SAY YOU ARE IN YOUR HOLY WORD.

I PRAISE YOU, FOR YOU MADE THIS BODY,

AND YOU CAN HEAL THIS BODY.

IN JESUS'S NAME I PRAY.

—FRAN LEFFLER

LORD, BE WITH MY FAMILY,

FROM THE OLDEST TO THE YOUNGEST.

GROW OUR RELATIONSHIPS.

GROW OUR PATIENCE;

GROW OUR LOVE.

RESTORE OUR SOULS.

SHOWER US WITH GRACE

DURING TIMES OF TROUBLE.

WEAVE LOVE INTO THE FABRIC

OF OUR FAMILY. AMEN.

—PAT LAWRENCE

O GOD, MAKE YOUR
WORDS CLEAR TO ME,

AS CLEAR AS THE ICE IS.

MAKE YOUR **LOVE** BE LIKE
A COMPASS FOR ME,

TO GIVE ME DIRECTION.

MAKE YOUR **TRUTH** TO BE LIKE
A SIGNPOST TO ME,

TO BRING ME CLARITY.

MAKE YOUR **PEACE** A GUIDE
FOR MY DIRECTIONS.

MAKE YOUR **HOPE** A FLAG
THAT TELLS ME

THAT I AM WALKING BESIDE YOU.

CLEAR MY **MIND** OF ALL
THE DISTRACTIONS

THAT STEAL ME FROM YOU.

O GOD, **BLESS ME**
WITH CLARITY.
AMEN!

—ANONYMOUS

DEAR JESUS, HELP ME TO
SPREAD THY FRAGRANCE
EVERYWHERE I GO.
FLOOD MY SOUL WITH
THY SPIRIT AND LOVE.
PENETRATE AND POSSESS
MY WHOLE BEING
SO UTTERLY THAT ALL MY LIFE
IS A RADIANCE OF THINE.
SHINE THROUGH ME
AND BE SO IN ME THAT EVERY SOUL
I COME IN CONTACT WITH
MAY FEEL THY PRESENCE IN MY SOUL.
LET THEM LOOK UP AND SEE
NO LONGER ME, BUT
ONLY JESUS.

—MOTHER TERESA

MY HEAVENLY FATHER,

WHEN MY SOUL WAS IN DESPAIR,

YOU WRAPPED ME IN YOUR LOVE.

YOU COMFORTED ME IN MY TIME OF LOSS.

AND I KNEW, TRULY KNEW,

THAT YOU ARE ALL I WILL EVER NEED.

—LILY KENT

GIVE THANKS TO THE LORD,

FOR HE IS GOOD.

HIS LOVE ENDURES FOREVER.

—PSALM 136:1

IF I AM NOT IN THE
STATE OF GRACE,
MAY GOD PUT ME THERE;
AND IF I AM,
MAY GOD SO KEEP ME.

—JOAN OF ARC

———

OUR REAL WORK
IS PRAYER.

—MOTHER MARIBEL

HEZEKIAH TURNED HIS FACE TO THE WALL
AND PRAYED TO THE LORD,
"REMEMBER, LORD, HOW I HAVE
WALKED BEFORE YOU FAITHFULLY
AND WITH WHOLEHEARTED DEVOTION
AND HAVE DONE WHAT IS GOOD
IN YOUR EYES."

—2 KINGS 20:2-3

FAR AWAY, THERE IN THE SUNSHINE,
ARE MY HIGHEST ASPIRATIONS.
I MAY NOT REACH THEM,
BUT I CAN LOOK UP AND SEE THEIR BEAUTY,
BELIEVE IN THEM, AND TRY TO FOLLOW
WHERE THEY LEAD.

—LOUISA MAY ALCOTT

HEAVENLY FATHER,
RIGHT NOW IT FEELS LIKE YOU ARE

MY LAST HOPE.

BUT THAT IS OKAY WITH ME,
BECAUSE YOU ARE ALSO

MY BEST HOPE!

—TAYLOR MORGAN

IT MAY SEEM A LITTLE OLD-FASHIONED,
ALWAYS TO BEGIN ONE'S WORK WITH PRAYER,
BUT I NEVER UNDERTAKE A HYMN
WITHOUT FIRST ASKING THE GOOD LORD
TO BE MY INSPIRATION.

—FANNY CROSBY

O LORD...
TAKE AWAY FROM ME
THE HEART OF STONE,
AND GIVE ME A HEART OF FLESH,
A HEART TO LOVE AND ADORE THEE,
A HEART TO DELIGHT IN THEE,
TO FOLLOW THEE AND ENJOY THEE,
FOR CHRIST'S SAKE.

—SAINT AMBROSE OF MILAN

———

WHAT IS IT YOU PLAN TO DO
WITH YOUR ONE WILD
AND PRECIOUS LIFE?

—MARY OLIVER

RICH

IS THE PERSON

WHO HAS A

PRAYING

FRIEND.

—JANICE HUGHES